The Return of the Druses by Robert Browning

A TRAGEDY

Bells and Pomegranates Number IV

The manuscript was first named Mansoor the Hierophant.

Robert Browning is one of the most significant Victorian Poets and, of course, English Poetry.

Much of his reputation is based upon his mastery of the dramatic monologue although his talents encompassed verse plays and even a well-regarded essay on Shelley during a long and prolific career.

He was born on May 7th, 1812 in Walmouth, London. Much of his education was home based and Browning was an eclectic and studious student, learning several languages and much else across a myriad of subjects, interests and passions.

Browning's early career began promisingly. The fragment from his intended long poem Pauline brought him to the attention of Dante Gabriel Rossetti, and was followed by Paracelsus, which was praised by both William Wordsworth and Charles Dickens. In 1840 the difficult Sordello, which was seen as willfully obscure, brought his career almost to a standstill.

Despite these artistic and professional difficulties his personal life was about to become immensely fulfilling. He began a relationship with, and then married, the older and better known Elizabeth Barrett. This new foundation served to energise his writings, his life and his career.

During their time in Italy they both wrote much of their best work. With her untimely death in 1861 he returned to London and thereafter began several further major projects.

The collection Dramatis Personae (1864) and the book-length epic poem The Ring and the Book (1868-69) were published and well received; his reputation as a venerated English poet now assured.

Robert Browning died in Venice on December 12th, 1889.

Index of Contents

PERSONS

The Grand-Master's Prefect.
The Patriarch's Nuncio.
The Republic's Admiral.
LOYS DE DREUX, Knight-Novice.
Initiated Druses—DJABAL, KHALIL, ANAEL, MAANI, KARSHOOK, RAGHIB,
AYOOB, and others.
Uninitiated Druses, Prefect's Guard, Nuncio's Attendants, Admiral's Force.

TIME: 14—.

PLACE: An Islet of the Southern Sporades, colonised by Druses of Lebanon, and garrisoned by the
Knights-Hospitallers of Rhodes.

SCENE: A Hall in the Prefect's Palace.

ACT I

Enter stealthily **KARSHOOK**, **RAGHIB**, **AYOOB**, and other initiated Druses, each as he enters casting off a
robe that conceals his distinctive black vest and white turban; then, as giving a loose to exultation,—

KARSHOOK
The moon is carried off in purple fire:
Day breaks at last! Break glory, with the day,
On Djabal's dread incarnate mystery
Now ready to resume its pristine shape
Of Hakeem, as the Khalif vanished erst
In what seemed death to uninstructed eyes,
On red Mokattam's verge—our Founder's flesh,
As he resumes our Founder's function!

RAGHIB
—Death
Sweep to the Christian Prefect that enslaved
So long us sad Druse exiles o'er the sea!

AYOOB
—Most joy be thine, O Mother-mount! Thy brood
Returns to thee, no outcasts as we left,
But thus—but thus! Behind, our Prefect's corse;
Before, a presence like the morning—thine,
Absolute Djabal late,—God Hakeem now
That day breaks!

KARSHOOK

Off then, with disguise at last!
As from our forms this hateful garb we strip,
Lose every tongue its glozing accent too,
Discard each limb the ignoble gesture! Cry,
'Tis the Druse Nation, warders on our Mount
Of the world's secret, since the birth of time,
—No kindred slips, no offsets from thy stock,
No spawn of Christians are we, Prefect, we
Who rise ...

AYOOB
Who shout ...

RAGHIB
Who seize, a first-fruits, ha—
Spoil of the spoiler! Brave!

[They begin to tear down, and to dispute for, the decorations of the hall.

KARSHOOK
Hold!

AYOOB
—Mine, I say;
And mine shall it continue!

KARSHOOK
Just this fringe!
Take anything beside! Lo, spire on spire,
Curl serpentwise wreathed columns to the top
O' the roof, and hide themselves mysteriously
Among the twinkling lights and darks that haunt
Yon cornice! Where the huge veil, they suspend
Before the Prefect's chamber of delight,
Floats wide, then falls again as if its slave,
The scented air, took heart now, and anon
Lost heart to buoy its breadths of gorgeousness
Above the gloom they droop in—all the porch
Is jewelled o'er with frostwork charactery;
And, see, yon eight-point cross of white flame, winking
Hoar-silvery like some fresh-broke marble stone:
Raze out the Rhodian cross there, so thou leav'st me
This single fringe!

AYOOB
Ha, wouldst thou, dog-fox? Help!
—Three hand-breadths of gold fringe, my son was set
To twist, the night he died!

KARSHOOK
Nay, hear the knave!
And I could witness my one daughter borne,
A week since, to the Prefect's couch, yet fold
These arms, be mute, lest word of mine should mar
Our Master's work, delay the Prefect here
A day, prevent his sailing hence for Rhodes—
How know I else?—Hear me denied my right
By such a knave!

RAGHIB [Interposing]
Each ravage for himself!
Booty enough! On, Druses! Be there found
Blood and a heap behind us; with us, Djabal
Turned Hakeem; and before us, Lebanon!
Yields the porch? Spare not! There his minions dragged
Thy daughter, Karshook, to the Prefect's couch!
Ayoob! Thy son, to soothe the Prefect's pride,
Bent o'er that task, the death-sweat on his brow,
Carving the spice-tree's heart in scroll-work there!
Onward in Djabal's name!

[As the tumult is at height, enter **KHALIL**. A pause and silence.

KHALIL
Was it for this,
Djabal hath summoned you? Deserve you thus
A portion in to-day's event? What, here—
When most behoves your feet fall soft, your eyes
Sink low, your tongues lie still,—at Djabal's side,
Close in his very hearing, who, perchance,
Assumes e'en now God Hakeem's dreaded shape,—
Dispute you for these gauds?

AYOOB
How say'st thou, Khalil?
Doubtless our Master prompts thee! Take the fringe,
Old Karshook! I supposed it was a day ...

KHALIL
For pillage?

KARSHOOK
Hearken, Khalil! Never spoke
A boy so like a song-bird; we avouch thee
Prettiest of all our Master's instruments
Except thy bright twin-sister; thou and Anael

Challenge his prime regard: but we may crave
(Such nothings as we be) a portion too
Of Djabal's favor; in him we believed,
His bound ourselves, him moon by moon obeyed,
Kept silence till this daybreak—so, may claim
Reward: who grudges me my claim?

AYOOB
To-day
Is not as yesterday!

RAGHIB
Stand off!

KHALIL
Rebel you?
Must I, the delegate of Djabal, draw
His wrath on you, the day of our Return?

OTHER DRUSES
Wrench from their grasp the fringe! Hounds! Must the earth
Vomit her plagues on us through thee?—and thee?
Plague me not, Khalil, for their fault!

KHALIL
Oh, shame!
Thus breaks to-day on you, the mystic tribe
Who, flying the approach of Osman, bore
Our faith, a merest spark, from Syria's ridge,
Its birthplace, hither! "Let the sea divide
These hunters from their prey," you said; "and safe
In this dim islet's virgin solitude
Tend we our faith, the spark, till happier time
Fan it to fire; till Hakeem rise again,
According to his word that, in the flesh
Which faded on Mokattam ages since,
He, at our extreme need, would interpose,
And, reinstating all in power and bliss,
Lead us himself to Lebanon once more."
Was't not thus you departed years ago,
Ere I was born?

OTHER DRUSES
'T was even thus, years ago.

KHALIL
And did you call—(according to old laws
Which bid us, lest the sacred grow profane,

Assimilate ourselves in outward rites
With strangers fortune makes our lords, and live
As Christian with the Christian, Jew with Jew
Druse only with the Druses)—did you call
Or no, to stand 'twixt you and Osman's rage,
(Mad to pursue e'en hither through the sea
The remnant of our tribe,) a race self vowed
To endless warfare with his hordes and him,
The White-cross Knights of the adjacent Isle?

KARSHOOK
And why else rend we down, wrench up, rase out?
These Knights of Rhodes we thus solicited
For help, bestowed on us a fiercer pest
Than aught we fled—their Prefect; who began
His promised mere paternal governance,
By a prompt massacre of all our Sheikhs
Able to thwart the Order in its scheme
Of crushing, with our nation's memory,
Each chance of our return, and taming us
Bondslaves to Rhodes forever—all, he thinks
To end by this day's treason.

KHALIL
Say I not?
You, fitted to the Order's purposes,
Your Sheikhs cut off, your rights, your garb proscribed,
Must yet receive one degradation more;
The Knights at last throw off the mask—transfer,
As tributary now and appanage,
This islet they are but protectors of,
To their own ever-craving liege, the Church,
Who licenses all crimes that pay her thus.
You, from their Prefect, were to be consigned
(Pursuant of I know not what vile pact)
To the Knights' Patriarch, ardent to outvie
His predecessor in all wickedness.
When suddenly rose Djabal in the midst,
Djabal, the man in semblance, but our God
Confessed by signs and portents. Ye saw fire
Bicker round Djabal, heard strange music flit
Bird-like about his brow?

OTHER DRUSES
We saw—we heard!
Djabal is Hakeem, the incarnate Dread,
The phantasm Khalif, King of Prodigies!

KHALIL
And as he said has not our Khalif done,
And so disposed events (from land to land
Passing invisibly) that when, this morn,
The pact of villany complete, there comes
This Patriarch's Nuncio with this Master's Prefect
Their treason to consummate,—each will face
For a crouching handful, an uplifted nation;
For simulated Christians, confessed Druses;
And, for slaves past hope of the Mother-mount,
Freedmen returning there 'neath Venice' flag;
That Venice which, the Hospitallers' foe,
Grants us from Candia escort home at price
Of our relinquished isle, Rhodes counts her own—
Venice, whose promised argosies should stand
Toward harbor: is it now that you, and you,
And you, selected from the rest to bear
The burden of the Khalif's secret, further
To-day's event, entitled by your wrongs,
And witness in the Prefect's hall his fate—
That you dare clutch these gauds? Ay, drop them!

KARSHOOK
True,
Most true, all this; and yet, may one dare hint,
Thou art the youngest of us?—though employed
Abundantly as Djabal's confidant,
Transmitter of his mandates, even now.
Much less, whene'er beside him Anael graces
The cedar throne, his queen-bride, art thou like
To occupy its lowest step that day!
Now, Khalil, wert thou checked as thou aspirest,
Forbidden such or such an honor,—say,
Would silence serve so amply?

KHALIL
Karshook thinks
I covet honors? Well, nor idly thinks!
Honors? I have demanded of them all
The greatest!

KARSHOOK
I supposed so.

KHALIL
Judge, yourselves!
Turn, thus: 'tis in the alcove at the back
Of yonder columned porch, whose entrance now

The veil hides, that our Prefect holds his state,
Receives the Nuncio, when the one, from Rhodes,
The other lands from Syria; there they meet.
Now, I have sued with earnest prayers ...

KARSHOOK
For what
Shall the Bride's brother vainly sue?

KHALIL
That mine—
Avenging in one blow a myriad wrongs
—Might be the hand to slay the Prefect there!
Djabal reserves that office for himself.

[A silence.

Thus far, as youngest of you all, I speak
—Scarce more enlightened than yourselves; since, near
As I approach him, nearer as I trust
Soon to approach our Master, he reveals
Only the God's power, not the glory yet.
Therefore I reasoned with you: now, as servant
To Djabal, bearing his authority,
Hear me appoint your several posts! Till noon
None see him save myself and Anael: once
The deed achieved, our Khalif, casting off
The embodied Awe's tremendous mystery,
The weakness of the flesh disguise, resumes
His proper glory, ne'er to fade again.

[Enter a **DRUSE**.

THE DRUSE
Our Prefect lands from Rhodes!—without a sign
That he suspects aught since he left our Isle;
Nor in his train a single guard beyond
The few he sailed with hence: so have we learned
From Loys.

KARSHOOK
Loys? Is not Loys gone
Forever?

AYOOB
Loys, the Frank Knight, returned?

The Druse. Loys, the boy, stood on the leading prow

Conspicuous in his gay attire, and leapt
Into the surf the foremost. Since day-dawn
I kept watch to the Northward; take but note
Of my poor vigilance to Djabal!

KHALIL
Peace!
Thou, Karshook, with thy company, receive
The Prefect as appointed: see, all keep
The wonted show of servitude: announce
His entry here by the accustomed peal
Of trumpets, then await the further pleasure
Of Djabal! (Loys back, whom Djabal sent
To Rhodes that we might spare the single Knight
Worth sparing!)

[Enter a **SECOND DRUSE**.

THE DRUSE
I espied it first! Say, I
First spied the Nuncio's galley from the South!
Said'st thou a Crossed-keys' flag would flap the mast?
It nears apace! One galley and no more.
If Djabal chance to ask who spied the flag,
Forget not, I it was!

KHALIL
Thou, Ayoob, bring
The Nuncio and his followers hither! Break
One rule prescribed, ye wither in your blood,
Die at your fault!

[Enter a **THIRD DRUSE**.

THE DRUSE
I shall see home, see home!
—Shall banquet in the sombre groves again!
Hail to thee, Khalil! Venice looms afar;
The argosies of Venice, like a cloud,
Bear up from Candia in the distance!

KHALIL
Joy!
Summon our people, Raghib! Bid all forth!
Tell them the long-kept secret, old and young!
Set free the captive, let the trampled raise
Their faces from the dust, because at length
The cycle is complete, God Hakeem's reign

Begins anew! Say, Venice for our guard,
Ere night we steer for Syria! Hear you, Druses?
Hear you this crowning witness to the claims
Of Djabal? Oh, I spoke of hope and fear,
Reward and punishment, because he bade
Who has the right: for me, what should I say
But, mar not those imperial lineaments,
No majesty of all that rapt regard
Vex by the least omission! Let him rise
Without a check from you!

OTHER DRUSES
Let Djabal rise!

[Enter **LOYS**.—The **DRUSES** are silent.

LOYS
Who speaks of Djabal?—for I seek him, friends!
[Aside.] Tu Dieu! 'T is as our Isle broke out in song
For joy, its Prefect-incubus drops off
To-day, and I succeed him in his rule!
But no—they cannot dream of their good fortune!
[Aloud.] Peace to you, Druses! I have tidings for you,
But first for Djabal: where 's your tall bewitcher,
With that small Arab thin-lipped silver-mouth?

KHALIL [Aside to **KARSHOOK**]
Loys, in truth! Yet Djabal cannot err!

KARSHOOK [To **KHALIL**]
And who takes charge of Loys? That 's forgotten,
Despite thy wariness! Will Loys stand
And see his comrades slaughtered?

LOYS [Aside]
How they shrink
And whisper, with those rapid faces! What?
The sight of me in their oppressors' garb
Strikes terror to the simple tribe? God's shame
On those that bring our Order ill repute!
But all's at end now; better days begin
For these mild mountaineers from over-sea:
The timidest shall have in me no Prefect
To cower at thus! [Aloud.] I asked for Djabal—

KARSHOOK [Aside]
Better
One lured him, ere he can suspect, inside

The corridor; 't were easy to dispatch
A youngster.
[To **LOYS**]
Djabal passed some minutes since
Through yonder porch, and ...

KHALIL [Aside]
Hold! What, him dispatch?
The only Christian of them all we charge
No tyranny upon? Who,—noblest Knight
Of all that learned from time to time their trade
Of lust and cruelty among us,—heir
To Europe's pomp, a truest child of pride,—
Yet stood between the Prefect and ourselves
From the beginning? Loys, Djabal makes
Account of, and precisely sent to Rhodes
For safety? I take charge of him!
[To **LOYS**]
Sir Loys,—

LOYS
There, cousins! Does Sir Loys strike you dead?

KHALIL [Advancing]
Djabal has intercourse with few or none
Till noontide: but, your pleasure?

LOYS
"Intercourse
With few or none?"—(Ah, Khalil, when you spoke
I saw not your smooth face! All health!—and health
To Anael! How fares Anael?)—"Intercourse
With few or none?" Forget you, I've been friendly
With Djabal long ere you or any Druse?
—Enough of him at Rennes, I think, beneath
The Duke my father's roof! He'd tell by the hour,
With fixed white eyes beneath his swarthy brow,
Plausiblest stories ...

KHALIL
Stories, say you?—Ah,
The quaint attire!

LOYS
My dress for the last time!
How sad I cannot make you understand,
This ermine, o'er a shield, betokens me
Of Bretagne, ancientest of provinces

And noblest; and, what's best and oldest there,
See, Dreux', our house's blazon, which the Nuncio
Tacks to an Hospitaller's vest to-day!

KHALIL

The Nuncio we await? What brings you back
From Rhodes, Sir Loys?

LOYS

How you island-tribe
Forget the world's awake while here you drowse!
What brings me back? What should not bring me, rather!
Our Patriarch's Nuncio visits you to-day—
Is not my year's probation out? I come
To take the knightly vows.

KHALIL

What's that you wear?

LOYS

This Rhodian cross? The cross your Prefect wore.
You should have seen, as I saw, the full Chapter
Rise, to a man, while they transferred this cross
From that unworthy Prefect's neck to ... (fool—
My secret will escape me!) In a word,
My year's probation passed, a Knight ere eve
Am I; bound, like the rest, to yield my wealth
To the common stock, to live in chastity,
(We Knights espouse alone our Order's fame)
—Change this gay weed for the black white-crossed gown,
And fight to death against the Infidel
—Not, therefore, against you, you Christians with
Such partial difference only as befits
The peacefullest of tribes. But Khalil, prithee,
Is not the Isle brighter than wont to-day?

KHALIL

Ah, the new sword!

LOYS

See now! You handle sword
As 't were a camel-staff! Pull! That's my motto,
Annealed "Pro fide," on the blade in blue.

KHALIL

No curve in it? Surely a blade should curve.

LOYS

Straight from the wrist! Loose—it should poise itself!

KHALIL [Waving with irrepressible exultation the sword]
We are a nation, Loys, of old fame
Among the mountains! Rights have we to keep
With the sword too!
[Remembering himself]
But I forget—you bid me
Seek Djabal?

LOYS
What! A sword's sight scares you not?
(The People I will make of him and them!
Oh let my Prefect-sway begin at once!)
Bring Djabal—say, indeed, that come he must!

KHALIL
At noon seek Djabal in the Prefect's Chamber,
And find ... [Aside] Nay, 't is thy cursed race's token,
Frank pride, no special insolence of thine!
[Aloud] Tarry, and I will do your bidding, Loys!
[To the **REST** aside] Now, forth you! I proceed to Djabal straight.
Leave this poor boy, who knows not what he says!
Oh will it not add joy to even thy joy,
Djabal, that I report all friends were true?

[**KHALIL** goes, followed by the **DRUSES**.

LOYS
Tu Dieu! How happy I shall make these Druses!
Was 't not surpassingly contrived of me
To get the long list of their wrongs by heart,
Then take the first pretence for stealing off
From these poor islanders, present myself
Sudden at Rhodes before the noble Chapter,
And (as best proof of ardor in its cause
Which ere to-night will have become, too, mine)
Acquaint it with this plague-sore in its body,
This Prefect and his villanous career?
The princely Synod! All I dared request
Was his dismissal; and they graciously
Consigned his very office to myself—
Myself may cure the Isle diseased!
And well
For them, they did so! Since I never felt
How lone a lot, though brilliant, I embrace,
Till now that, past retrieval, it is mine.
To live thus, and thus die! Yet, as I leapt

On shore, so home a feeling greeted me
That I could half believe in Djabal's story,
He used to tempt my father with, at Rennes—
And me, too, since the story brought me here—
Of some Count Dreux and ancestor of ours
Who, sick of wandering from Bouillon's war,
Left his old name in Lebanon.
Long days
At least to spend in the Isle! and, my news known
An hour hence, what if Anael turn on me
The great black eyes I must forget?
Why, fool,
Recall them, then? My business is with Djabal,
Not Anael! Djabal tarries: if I seek him?—
The Isle is brighter than its wont to-day!

ACT II

Enter **DJABAL**.

DJABAL
That a strong man should think himself a God!
I—Hakeem? To have wandered through the world,
Sown falsehood, and thence reaped now scorn, now faith,
For my one chant with many a change, my tale
Of outrage, and my prayer for vengeance—this
Required, forsooth, no mere man's faculty,
Naught less than Hakeem's? The persuading Loys
To pass probation here: the getting access
By Loys to the Prefect; worst of all,
The gaining my tribe's confidence by fraud
That would disgrace the very Frank,—a few
Of Europe's secrets which subdue the flame,
The wave,—to ply a simple tribe with these,
Took Hakeem?
And I feel this first to-day!
Does the day break, is the hour imminent
When one deed, when my whole life's deed, my deed
Must be accomplished? Hakeem? Why the God?
Shout, rather, "Djabal, Youssof's child, thought slain
With his whole race, the Druses' Sheikhs, this Prefect
Endeavored to extirpate—saved, a child,
Returns from traversing the world, a man,
Able to take revenge, lead back the march
To Lebanon"—so shout, and who gainsays?
But now, because delusion mixed itself

Insensibly with this career, all 's changed!
Have I brought Venice to afford us convoy?
"True—but my jugglings wrought that!" Put I heart
Into our people where no heart lurked?—"Ah,
What cannot an impostor do!"
Not this!
Not do this which I do! Not bid avaunt
Falsehood! Thou shalt not keep thy hold on me!
—Nor even get a hold on me! 'T is now—
This day—hour—minute—'t is as here I stand
On the accursed threshold of the Prefect,
That I am found deceiving and deceived!
And now what do I?—hasten to the few
Deceived, ere they deceive the many—shout,
"As I professed, I did believe myself!
Say, Druses, had you seen a butchery—
If Ayoob, Karshook saw——Maani there
Must tell you how I saw my father sink;
My mother's arms twine still about my neck;
I hear my brother shriek, here's yet the scar
Of what was meant for my own death-blow—say,
If you had woke like me, grown year by year
Out of the tumult in a far-off clime,
Would it be wondrous such delusion grew?
I walked the world, asked help at every hand;
Came help or no? Not this and this? Which helps
When I returned with, found the Prefect here,
The Druses here, all here but Hakeem's self,
The Khalif of the thousand prophecies,
Reserved for such a juncture,—could I call
My mission aught but Hakeem's? Promised Hakeem
More than performs the Djabal—you absolve?
—Me, you will never shame before the crowd
Yet happily ignorant?—Me, both throngs surround,
The few deceived, the many unabused,
—Who, thus surrounded, slay for you and them
The Prefect, lead to Lebanon? No Khalif,
But Sheikh once more! Mere Djabal—not" ...

[Enter **KHALIL** hastily.

KHALIL
—God Hakeem!
'T is told! The whole Druse nation knows thee, Hakeem,
As we! and mothers lift on high their babes
Who seem aware, so glisten their great eyes,
Thou hast not failed us; ancient brows are proud;
Our elders could not earlier die, it seems,

Than at thy coming! The Druse heart is thine!
Take it! my lord and theirs, be thou adored!

DJABAL [Aside]
Adored!—but I renounce it utterly!

KHALIL
Already are they instituting choirs
And dances to the Khalif, as of old
'T is chronicled thou bad'st them.

DJABAL [Aside]
I abjure it!
'T is not mine—not for me!

KHALIL
Why pour they wine
Flavored like honey and bruised mountain-herbs,
Or wear those strings of sun-dried cedar-fruit?
Oh, let me tell thee—Esaad, we supposed
Doting, is carried forth, eager to see
The last sun rise on the Isle: he can see now!
The shamed Druse women never wept before:
They can look up when we reach home, they say.
Smell!—sweet cane, saved in Lilith's breast thus long—
Sweet!—it grows wild in Lebanon. And I
Alone do nothing for thee! 'T is my office
Just to announce what well thou know'st—but thus
Thou bidst me. At this self-same moment tend
The Prefect, Nuncio and the Admiral
Hither by their three sea-paths: nor forget
Who were the trusty watchers!—thou forget?
Like me, who do forget that Anael bade ...

DJABAL [Aside]
Ay, Anael, Anael—is that said at last?
Louder than all, that would be said, I knew!
What does abjuring mean, confessing mean,
To the people? Till that woman crossed my path,
On went I, solely for my people's sake:
I saw her, and I then first saw myself,
And slackened pace: "If I should prove indeed
Hakeem—with Anael by!"

KHALIL [Aside]
Ah, he is rapt!
Dare I at such a moment break on him
Even to do my sister's bidding? Yes:

The eyes are Djabal's and not Hakeem's yet,
Though but till I have spoken this, perchance.

DJABAL [Aside]
To yearn to tell her, and yet have no one
Great heart's word that will tell her! I could gasp
Doubtless one such word out, and die.
[Aloud]
You said
That Anael ...

KHALIL
... Fain would see thee, speak with thee,
Before thou change, discard this Djabal's shape
She knows, for Hakeem's shape she is to know.
Something to say that will not from her mind!
I know not what—"Let him but come!" she said.

DJABAL [Half apart]
My nation—all my Druses—how fare they?
Those I must save, and suffer thus to save,
Hold they their posts? Wait they their Khalif too?

KHALIL
All at the signal pant to flock around
That banner of a brow!

DJABAL [Aside]
And when they flock,
Confess them this: and after, for reward,
Be chased with howlings to her feet perchance!
—Have the poor outraged Druses, deaf and blind,
Precede me there, forestall my story there,
Tell it in mocks and jeers!
I lose myself!
Who needs a Hakeem to direct him now?
I need the veriest child—why not this child?

[Turning abruptly to **KHALIL**.

You are a Druse too, Khalil; you were nourished
Like Anael with our mysteries: if she
Could vow, so nourished, to love only one
Who should avenge the Druses, whence proceeds
Your silence? Wherefore made you no essay,
Who thus implicitly can execute
My bidding? What have I done, you could not?
Who, knowing more than Anael the prostration

Of our once lofty tribe, the daily life
Of this detested ...
Does he come, you say,
This Prefect? All's in readiness?

KHALIL
The sword,
The sacred robe, the Khalif's mystic tiar,
Laid up so long, are all disposed beside
The Prefect's chamber.

DJABAL
—Why did you despair?

KHALIL
I know our nation's state? Too surely know,
As thou who speak'st to prove me! Wrongs like ours
Should wake revenge: but when I sought the wronged
And spoke,—"The Prefect stabbed your son— arise!
Your daughter, while you starve, eats shameless bread
In his pavilion—then arise!"—my speech
Fell idly: 't was, "Be silent, or worse fare!
Endure till time 's slow cycle prove complete!
Who may'st thou be that takest on thee to thrust
Into this peril—art thou Hakeem?" No!
Only a mission like thy mission renders
All these obedient at a breath, subdues
Their private passions, brings their wills to one!

DJABAL
You think so?

KHALIL
Even now—when they have witnessed
Thy miracles—had I not threatened all
With Hakeem's vengeance, they would mar the work,
And couch ere this, each with his special prize,
Safe in his dwelling, leaving our main hope
To perish. No! When these have kissed thy feet
At Lebanon, the past purged off, the present
Clear,—for the future, even Hakeem's mission
May end, and I perchance, or any youth,
Shall rule them thus renewed.—I tutor thee!

DJABAL
And wisely. (He is Anael's brother, pure
As Anael's self.) Go say, I come to her.
Haste! I will follow you.

[**KHALIL** goes.

Oh, not confess
To these, the blinded multitude—confess,
Before at least the fortune of my deed
Half authorize its means! Only to her
Let me confess my fault, who in my path
Curled up like incense from a Mage-king's tomb
When he would have the wayfarer descend
Through the earth's rift and bear hid treasure forth!
How should child's-carelessness prove manhood's crime
Till now that I, whose lone youth hurried past,
Letting each joy 'scape for the Druses' sake,
At length recover in one Druse all joy?
Were her brow brighter, her eyes richer, still
Would I confess! On the gulf's verge I pause.
How could I slay the Prefect, thus and thus?
Anael, be mine to guard me, not destroy!

[Goes.

[Enter **ANAEL**, and **MAANI** who is assisting to array her in the ancient dress of the Druses.

ANAEL
Those saffron vestures of the tabret-girls!
Comes Djabal, think you?

MAANI
Doubtless Djabal comes.

ANAEL
Dost thou snow-swathe thee kinglier, Lebanon,
Than in my dreams?—Nay, all the tresses off
My forehead! Look I lovely so? He says
That I am lovely.

MAANI
Lovely: nay, that hangs
Awry.

ANAEL
You tell me how a khandjar hangs?
The sharp side, thus, along the heart, see, marks
The maiden of our class. Are you content
For Djabal as for me?

MAANI

Content, my child.

ANAEL

Oh mother, tell me more of him! He comes
Even now—tell more, fill up my soul with him!

MAANI

And did I not … yes, surely … tell you all?

ANAEL

What will be changed in Djabal when the Change
Arrives? Which feature? Not his eyes!

MAANI

'T is writ
Our Hakeem's eyes rolled fire and clove the dark
Superbly.

ANAEL

Not his eyes! His voice perhaps?
Yet that's no change; for a grave current lived
—Grandly beneath the surface ever lived,
That, scattering, broke as in live silver spray
While … ah, the bliss … he would discourse to me
In that enforced still fashion, word on word!
'T is the old current which must swell through that,
For what least tone, Maani, could I lose?
'T is surely not his voice will change!
—If Hakeem
Only stood by! If Djabal, somehow, passed
Out of the radiance as from out a robe;
Possessed, but was not it!
He lived with you?
Well—and that morning Djabal saw me first
And heard me vow never to wed but one
Who saved my People—on that day … proceed!

MAANI

Once more, then: from the time of his return
In secret, changed so since he left the Isle
That I, who screened our Emir's last of sons,
This Djabal, from the Prefect's massacre
—Who bade him ne'er forget the child he was,
—Who dreamed so long the youth he might become—
I knew not in the man that child; the man
Who spoke alone of hope to save our tribe,
How he had gone from land to land to save
Our tribe—allies were sure, nor foes to dread;

And much he mused, days, nights, alone he mused:
But never till that day when, pale and worn
As by a persevering woe, he cried
"Is there not one Druse left me?"—and I showed
The way to Khalil's and your hiding-place
From the abhorred eye of the Prefect here,
So that he saw you, heard you speak—till then,
Never did he announce—(how the moon seemed
To ope and shut, the while, above us both!)
—His mission was the mission promised us;
The cycle had revolved; all things renewing,
He was lost Hakeem clothed in flesh to lead
His children home anon, now veiled to work
Great purposes: the Druses now would change!

ANAEL
And they have changed! And obstacles did sink,
And furtherances rose! And round his form
Played fire, and music beat her angel wings!
My people, let me more rejoice, oh more
For you than for myself! Did I but watch
Afar the pageant, feel our Khalif pass,
One of the throng, how proud were I—though ne'er
Singled by Djabal's glance! But to be chosen
His own from all, the most his own of all,
To be exalted with him, side by side,
Lead the exulting Druses, meet ... ah, how
Worthily meet the maidens who await
Ever beneath the cedars—how deserve
This honor, in their eyes? So bright are they
Who saffron-vested sound the tabret there,
The girls who throng there in my dream! One hour
And all is over: how shall I do aught
That may deserve next hour's exalting?—
How?—
[Suddenly to **MAANI**.
Mother, I am not worthy him! I read it
Still in his eyes! He stands as if to tell me
I am not, yet forbears. Why else revert
To one theme ever?—how mere human gifts
Suffice him in myself—whose worship fades,
Whose awe goes ever off at his approach,
As now, who when he comes ...

[**DJABAL** enters.

Oh why is it
I cannot kneel to you?

DJABAL
Rather, 't is I
Should kneel to you, my Anael!

ANAEL
Even so!
For never seem you—shall I speak the truth?—
Never a God to me! 'T is the Man's hand,
Eye, voice! Oh, do you veil these to our people,
Or but to me? To them, I think, to them!
And brightness is their veil, shadow—my truth!
You mean that I should never kneel to you
—So, thus I kneel!

DJABAL [Preventing her]
No—no!

[Feeling the khandjar as he raises her.

Ha, have you chosen ...

ANAEL
The khandjar with our ancient garb. But, Djabal,
Change not, be not exalted yet! Give time
That I may plan more, perfect more! My blood
Beats, beats!
[Aside.] Oh, must I then—since Loys leaves us
Never to come again, renew in me
These doubts so near effaced already—must
I needs confess them now to Djabal?—own
That when I saw that stranger, heard his voice,
My faith fell, and the woeful thought flashed first
That each effect of Djabal's presence, taken
For proof of more than human attributes
In him, by me whose heart at his approach
Beat fast, whose brain while he was by swam round,
Whose soul at his departure died away,
—That every such effect might have been wrought
In other frames, though not in mine, by Loys
Or any merely mortal presence? Doubt
Is fading fast: shall I reveal it now?
How shall I meet the rapture presently,
With doubt unexpiated, undisclosed?

DJABAL [Aside]
Avow the truth? I cannot! In what words
Avow that all she loved in me was false?

—Which yet has served that flower-like love of hers
To climb by, like the clinging gourd, and clasp
With its divinest wealth of leaf and bloom.
Could I take down the prop-work, in itself
So vile, yet interlaced and overlaid
With painted cups and fruitage—might these still
Bask in the sun, unconscious their own strength
Of matted stalk and tendril had replaced
The old support thus silently withdrawn!
But no; the beauteous fabric crushes too.
'T is not for my sake but for Anael's sake
I leave her soul this Hakeem where it leans.
Oh could I vanish from her, quit the Isle!
And yet—a thought comes: here my work is done
At every point; the Druses must return—
Have convoy to their birth-place back, whoe'er
The leader be, myself or any Druse—
Venice is pledged to that: 't is for myself,
For my own vengeance in the Prefect's death,
I stay now, not for them: to slay or spare
The Prefect, whom imports it save myself?
He cannot bar their passage from the Isle;
What would his death be but my own reward?
Then, mine I will forego. It is foregone!
Let him escape with all my House's blood!
Ere he can reach land, Djabal disappears,
And Hakeem, Anael loved, shall, fresh as first,
Live in her memory, keeping her sublime
Above the world. She cannot touch that world
By ever knowing what I truly am,
Since Loys,—of mankind the only one
Able to link my present with my past,
My life in Europe with my Island life,
Thence, able to unmask me,—I 've disposed
Safely at last at Rhodes, and ...

[Enter **KHALIL**.

KHALIL
Loys greets thee!

DJABAL
Loys? To drag me back? It cannot be!

ANAEL [Aside]
Loys! Ah, doubt may not be stifled so!

KHALIL

Can I have erred that thou so gazest? Yes,
I told thee not in the glad press of tidings
Of higher import, Loys is returned
Before the Prefect, with, if possible,
Twice the light-heartedness of old. As though
On some inauguration he expects,
To-day, the world's fate hung!

DJABAL
—And asks for me?

KHALIL
Thou knowest all things. Thee in chief he greets,
But every Druse of us is to be happy
At his arrival, he declares: were Loys
Thou, Master, he could have no wider soul
To take us in with. How I love that Loys!

DJABAL [Aside]
Shame winds me with her tether round and round!

ANAEL [Aside]
Loys? I take the trial! it is meet,
The little I can do, be done; that faith,
All I can offer, want no perfecting
Which my own act may compass. Ay, this way
All may go well, nor that ignoble doubt
Be chased by other aid than mine. Advance
Close to my fear, weigh Loys with my Lord,
The mortal with the more than mortal gifts!

DJABAL [Aside]
Before, there were so few deceived! and now
There's doubtless not one least Druse in the Isle
But, having learned my superhuman claims,
And calling me his Khalif-God, will clash
The whole truth out from Loys at first word!
While Loys, for his part, will hold me up,
With a Frank's unimaginable scorn
Of such imposture, to my people's eyes!
Could I but keep him longer yet awhile
From them, amuse him here until I plan
How he and I at once may leave the Isle!
Khalil I cannot part with from my side—
My only help in this emergency:
There's Anael!

ANAEL

Please you?

DJABAL
Anael—none but she!
[To **ANAEL**]
I pass some minutes in the chamber there,
Ere I see Loys: you shall speak with him
Until I join you. Khalil follows me.

ANAEL [Aside]
As I divined: he bids me save myself,
Offers me a probation—I accept!
Let me see Loys!

LOYS [Withou.]
Djabal!

ANAEL [Aside]
'Tis his voice.
The smooth Frank trifler with our people's wrongs,
The self-complacent boy-inquirer, loud
On this and that inflicted tyranny,
—Aught serving to parade an ignorance
Of how wrong feels, inflicted! Let me close
With what I viewed at distance: let myself
Probe this delusion to the core!

DJABAL
He comes.
Khalil, along with me! while Anael waits
Till I return once more—and but once more!

ACT III

ANAEL and **LOYS**.

ANAEL
Here leave me! Here I wait another. 'T was
For no mad protestation of a love
Like this you say possesses you, I came.

LOYS
Love? how protest a love I dare not feel?
Mad words may doubtless have escaped me: you
Are here—I only feel you here!

ANAEL
No more!

LOYS
But once again, whom could you love? I dare,
Alas, say nothing of myself, who am
A Knight now, for when Knighthood we embrace,
Love we abjure: so, speak on safely: speak,
Lest I speak, and betray my faith! And yet
To say your breathing passes through me, changes
My blood to spirit, and my spirit to you,
As Heaven the sacrificer's wine to it—
This is not to protest my love! You said
You could love one ...

ANAEL
One only! We are bent
To earth—who raises up my tribe, I love;
The Prefect bows us—who removes him; we
Have ancient rights—who gives them back to us,
I love. Forbear me! Let my hand go!

LOYS
Him
You could love only? Where is Djabal? Stay!
[Aside.] Yet wherefore stay? Who does this but myself?
Had I apprised her that I come to do
Just this, what more could she acknowledge? No,
She sees into my heart's core! What is it
Feeds either cheek with red, as June some rose?
Why turns she from me? Ah fool, over-fond
To dream I could call up ...

... What never dream
Yet feigned! 'Tis love! Oh Anael, speak to me!
Djabal—

ANAEL
Seek Djabal by the Prefect's chamber
At noon!

[She paces the room.

LOYS [Aside]
And am I not the Prefect now?
Is it my fate to be the only one
Able to win her love, the only one
Unable to accept her love? The past

Breaks up beneath my footing: came I here
This morn as to a slave, to set her free
And take her thanks, and then spend day by day
Content beside her in the Isle? What works
This knowledge in me now? Her eye has broken
The faint disguise away: for Anael's sake
I left the Isle, for her espoused the cause
Of the Druses, all for her I thought, till now,
To live without!
—As I must live! To-day
Ordains me Knight, forbids me ... never shall
Forbid me to profess myself, heart, arm,
Thy soldier!

ANAEL
Djabal you demanded, comes!

LOYS [Aside]
What wouldst thou, Loys? see him? Naught beside
Is wanting: I have felt his voice a spell
From first to last. He brought me here, made known
The Druses to me, drove me hence to seek
Redress for them; and shall I meet him now,
When naught is wanting but a word of his,
To—what?—induce me to spurn hope, faith, pride,
Honor away,—to cast my lot among
His tribe, become a proverb in men's mouths,
Breaking my high pact of companionship
With those who graciously bestowed on me
The very opportunities I turn
Against them! Let me not see Djabal now!

ANAEL
The Prefect also comes!

LOYS [Aside]
Him let me see,
Not Djabal! Him, degraded at a word,
To soothe me,—to attest belief in me—
And after, Djabal! Yes, ere I return
To her, the Nuncio's vow shall have destroyed
This heart's rebellion, and coerced this will
Forever.
Anael, not before the vows
Irrevocably fix me ...
Let me fly!
The Prefect, or I lose myself forever!

[Goes.

ANAEL
Yes, I am calm now; just one way remains—
One, to attest my faith in him: for, see,
I were quite lost else: Loys, Djabal, stand
On either side—two men! I balance looks
And words, give Djabal a man's preference,
No more. In Djabal, Hakeem is absorbed!
And for a love like this, the God who saves
My race, selects me for his bride? One way!—

[Enter **DJABAL**.

DJABAL [To himself]
No moment is to waste then; 'tis resolved.
If Khalil may be trusted to lead back
My Druses, and if Loys can be lured
Out of the Isle—if I procure his silence,
Or promise never to return at least,—
All's over. Even now my bark awaits:
I reach the next wild islet and the next,
And lose myself beneath the sun forever.
And now, to Anael!

ANAEL
Djabal, I am thine!

DJABAL
Mine? Djabal's?—As if Hakeem had not been?

ANAEL
Not Djabal's? Say first, do you read my thought?
Why need I speak, if you can read my thought?

DJABAL
I do not, I have said a thousand times.

ANAEL
(My secret's safe, I shall surprise him yet!)
Djabal, I knew your secret from the first:
Djabal, when first I saw you ... (by our porch
You leant, and pressed the tinkling veil away,
And one fringe fell behind your neck—I see!)
... I knew you were not human, for I said
"This dim secluded house where the sea beats
Is heaven to me—my people's huts are hell
To them; this august form will follow me,

Mix with the waves his voice will,—I have him;
And they, the Prefect! Oh, my happiness
Rounds to the full whether I choose or no!
His eyes met mine, he was about to speak,
His hand grew damp—surely he meant to say
He let me love him: in that moment's bliss
I shall forget my people pine for home—
They pass and they repass with pallid eyes!"
I vowed at once a certain vow; this vow—
Not to embrace you till my tribe was saved.
Embrace me!

DJABAL [Apart]
And she loved me! Naught remained
But that! Nay, Anael, is the Prefect dead?

ANAEL
Ah, you reproach me! True, his death crowns all,
I know—or should know: and I would do much,
Believe! but, death! Oh, you, who have known death,
Would never doom the Prefect, were death fearful
As we report!
Death!—a fire curls within us
From the foot's palm, and fills up to the brain,
Up, out, then shatters the whole bubble-shell
Of flesh, perchance!
Death!—witness, I would die,
Whate'er death be, would venture now to die
For Khalil, for Maani—what for thee?
Nay, but embrace me, Djabal, in assurance
My vow will not be broken, for I must
Do something to attest my faith in you,
Be worthy you!

DJABAL [Avoiding her]
I come for that—to say
Such an occasion is at hand: 'tis like
I leave you—that we part, my Anael,—part
Forever!

ANAEL
We part? Just so! I have succumbed,—
I am, he thinks, unworthy—and naught less
Will serve than such approval of my faith.
Then, we part not! Remains there no way short
Of that? Oh, not that!
Death!—yet a hurt bird
Died in my hands; its eyes filmed—"Nay, it sleeps,"

I said, "will wake to-morrow well:" 't was dead.

DJABAL
I stand here and time fleets. Anael—I come
To bid a last farewell to you: perhaps
We never meet again. But, ere the Prefect
Arrive ...

[Enter **KHALIL**, breathlessly.

KHALIL
He's here! The Prefect! Twenty guards,
No more—no sign he dreams of danger. All
Awaits thee only. Ayoob, Karshook, keep
Their posts—wait but the deed's accomplishment
To join us with thy Druses to a man.
Still holds his course the Nuncio—near and near
The fleet from Candia steering.

DJABAL [Aside]
All is lost!
—Or won?

KHALIL
And I have laid the sacred robe,
The sword, the head-tiar, at the porch—the place
Commanded. Thou wilt hear the Prefect's trumpet.

DJABAL
Then I keep Anael,—him then, past recall,
I slay—'tis forced on me! As I began
I must conclude—so be it!

KHALIL
For the rest,
Save Loys, our foe's solitary sword,
All is so safe that ... I will ne'er entreat
Thy post again of thee: though danger none,
There must be glory only meet for thee
In slaying the Prefect!

ANAEL [Aside]
And 'tis now that Djabal
Would leave me!—in the glory meet for him!

DJABAL
As glory, I would yield the deed to you
Or any Druse; what peril there may be,

I keep. [Aside.] All things conspire to hound me on!
Not now, my soul, draw back, at least! Not now!
The course is plain, howe'er obscure all else.
Once offer this tremendous sacrifice,
Prevent what else will be irreparable,
Secure these transcendental helps, regain
The Cedars—then let all dark clear itself!
I slay him!

KHALIL
Anael, and no part for us!
[To **DJABAL**]
Hast thou possessed her with ...

DJABAL [To **ANAEL**]
Whom speak you to?
What is it you behold there? Nay, this smile
Turns stranger. Shudder you? The man must die,
As thousands of our race have died through him.
One blow, and I discharge his weary soul
From the flesh that pollutes it! Let him fill
Straight some new expiatory form, of earth
Or sea, the reptile or some aëry thing:
What is there in his death?

ANAEL
My brother said,
Is there no part in it for us?

DJABAL
For Khalil,—
The trumpet will announce the Nuncio's entry;
Here, I shall find the Prefect hastening
In the Pavilion to receive him—here
I slay the Prefect; meanwhile Ayoob leads
The Nuncio with his guards within: once these
Secured in the outer hall, bid Ayoob bar
Entry or egress till I give the sign
Which waits the landing of the argosies
You will announce to me: this double sign
That justice is performed and help arrived,
When Ayoob shall receive, but not before,
Let him throw ope the palace doors, admit
The Druses to behold their tyrant, ere
We leave forever this detested spot.
Go, Khalil, hurry all! No pause, no pause!
Whirl on the dream, secure to wake anon!

KHALIL
What sign? and who the bearer?

DJABAL
Who shall show
My ring, admit to Ayoob. How she stands!
Have I not ... I must have some task for her.
Anael, not that way! 'T is the Prefect's chamber!
Anael, keep you the ring—give you the sign!
(It holds her safe amid the stir.) You will
Be faithful?

ANAEL [Taking the ring]
I would fain be worthy. Hark!

[Trumpet without.

KHALIL
He comes!

DJABAL
And I too come.

ANAEL
One word, but one!
Say, shall you be exalted at the deed?
Then? On the instant?

DJABAL
I exalted? What?
He, there—we, thus—our wrongs revenged, our tribe
Set free? Oh, then shall I, assure yourself,
Shall you, shall each of us, be in his death
Exalted!

KHALIL
He is here!

DJABAL
Away—away!

[They go.

[Enter the **PREFECT** with **GUARDS**, and **LOYS**.

THE PREFECT [To **GUARDS**]
Back, I say, to the galley every guard!
That's my sole care now; see each bench retains

Its complement of rowers; I embark
O' the instant, since this Knight will have it so.
Alas me! Could you have the heart, my Loys!
[To a **GUARD** who whispers]
Oh, bring the holy Nuncio here forthwith!

[The **GUARDS** go.

Loys, a rueful sight, confess, to see
The gray discarded Prefect leave his post,
With tears i' the eye! So, you are Prefect now?
You depose me—you succeed me? Ha, ha!

LOYS
And dare you laugh, whom laughter less becomes
Than yesterday's forced meekness we beheld ...

THE PREFECT
—When you so eloquently pleaded, Loys,
For my dismissal from the post? Ah, meek
With cause enough, consult the Nuncio else!
And wish him the like meekness: for so stanch
A servant of the church can scarce have bought
His share in the Isle, and paid for it, hard pieces!
You 've my successor to condole with, Nuncio!
I shall be safe by then i' the galley, Loys!

LOYS
You make as you would tell me you rejoice
To leave your scene of ...

THE PREFECT
Trade in the dear Druses?
Blood and sweat traffic? Spare what yesterday
We heard enough of! Drove I in the Isle
A profitable game? Learn wit, my son,
Which you'll need shortly! Did it never breed
Suspicion in you, all was not pure profit,
When I, the insatiate ... and so forth—was bent
On having a partaker in my rule?
Why did I yield this Nuncio half the gain,
If not that I might also shift—what on him?
Half of the peril, Loys!

LOYS
Peril?

THE PREFECT

Hark you!
I'd love you if you'd let me—this for reason,
You save my life at price of ... well, say risk
At least, of yours. I came a long time since
To the Isle; our Hospitallers bade me tame
These savage wizards, and reward myself—

LOYS
The Knights who so repudiate your crime?

THE PREFECT
Loys, the Knights! we doubtless understood
Each other; as for trusting to reward
From any friend beside myself ... no, no!
I clutched mine on the spot, when it was sweet,
And I had taste for it. I felt these wizards
Alive—was sure they were not on me, only
When I was on them: but with age comes caution:
And stinging pleasures please less and sting more.
Year by year, fear by fear! The girls were brighter
Than ever ('faith, there's yet one Anael left,
I set my heart upon—Oh, prithee, let
That brave new sword lie still!)—These joys looked brighter,
But silenter the town, too, as I passed.
With this alcove's delicious memories
Began to mingle visions of gaunt fathers,
Quick-eyed sons, fugitives from the mine, the oar,
Stealing to catch me. Brief, when I began
To quake with fear—(I think I hear the Chapter
Solicited to let me leave, now all
Worth staying for was gained and gone!)—I say.
Just when, for the remainder of my life,
All methods of escape seemed lost—that then
Up should a young hot-headed Loys spring,
Talk very long and loud,—in fine, compel
The Knights to break their whole arrangement, have me
Home for pure shame—from this safehold of mine
Where but ten thousand Druses seek my life,
To my wild place of banishment, San Gines
By Murcia, where my three fat manors lying,
Purchased by gains here and the Nuncio's gold,
Are all I have to guard me,—that such fortune
Should fall to me, I hardly could expect.
Therefore I say, I 'd love you.

LOYS
Can it be?
I play into your hands then? Oh no, no!

The Venerable Chapter, the Great Order
Sunk o' the sudden into fiends of the pit?
But I will back—will yet unveil you!

THE PREFECT
Me?
To whom?—perhaps Sir Galeas, who in Chapter
Shook his white head thrice—and some dozen times
My hand next morning shook, for value paid!
To that Italian saint, Sir Cosimo?—
Indignant at my wringing year by year
A thousand bezants from the coral divers,
As you recounted; felt the saint aggrieved
Well might he—I allowed for his half-share
Merely one hundred! To Sir ...

LOYS
See! you dare
Inculpate the whole Order; yet should I,
A youth, a sole voice, have the power to change
Their evil way, had they been firm in it?
Answer me!

THE PREFECT
Oh, the son of Bretagne's Duke,
And that son's wealth, the father's influence, too,
And the young arm, we'll even say, my Loys,
—The fear of losing or diverting these
Into another channel, by gainsaying
A novice too abruptly, could not influence
The Order! You might join, for aught they cared,
Their red-cross rivals of the Temple! Well,
I thank you for my part, at all events.
Stay here till they withdraw you! You'll inhabit
My palace—sleep, perchance, in the alcove
Whither I go to meet our holy friend.
Good! and now disbelieve me if you can,—
This is the first time for long years I enter
Thus

[lifts the arras.

—without feeling just as if I lifted
The lid up of my tomb.

LOYS
They share his crime!
God's punishment will overtake you yet.

THE PREFECT

Thank you it does not! Pardon this last flash:
I bear a sober visage presently
With the disinterested Nuncio here—
His purchase-money safe at Murcia, too!
Let me repeat—for the first time, no draught
Coming as from a sepulchre salutes me.
When we next meet, this folly may have passed,
We'll hope. Ha, ha!

[Goes through the arras.

LOYS

Assure me but ... he's gone!
He could not lie. Then what have I escaped,
I, who had so nigh given up happiness
Forever, to be linked with him and them!
Oh, opportunest of discoveries! I
Their Knight? I utterly renounce them all!
Hark! What, he meets by this the Nuncio? Yes,
The same hyæna groan-like laughter! Quick—
To Djabal! I am one of them at last,
These simple-hearted Druses—Anael's tribe!
Djabal! She's mine at last. Djabal, I say!

[Goes.

ACT IV

Enter **DJABAL**.

DJABAL

Let me but slay the Prefect. The end now!
To-morrow will be time enough to pry
Into the means I took: suffice, they served,
Ignoble as they were, to hurl revenge
True to its object.

[Seeing the robe, etc. disposed.

Mine should never so
Have hurried to accomplishment! Thee, Djabal,
Far other mood befitted! Calm the Robe
Should clothe this doom's awarder!

[Taking the robe.

Shall I dare
Assume my nation's Robe? I am at least
A Druse again, chill Europe's policy
Drops from me: I dare take the Robe. Why not
The Tiar? I rule the Druses, and what more
Betokens it than rule?—yet—yet—

[Lays down the tiar.

[Footsteps in the alcove.

He comes!

[Taking the sword.

If the Sword serve, let the Tiar lie! So, feet
Clogged with the blood of twenty years can fall
Thus lightly! Round me, all ye ghosts! He'll lift ...
Which arm to push the arras wide?—or both?
Stab from the neck down to the heart—there stay!
Near he comes—nearer—the next footstep! Now!

[As he dashes aside the arras, **ANAEL** is discovered.

Ha! Anael! Nay, my Anael, can it be?
Heard you the trumpet? I must slay him here,
And here you ruin all. Why speak you not?
Anael, the Prefect comes!

[**ANAEL** screams.

So slow to feel
'T is not a sight for you to look upon?
A moment's work—but such work! Till you go,
I must be idle—idle, I risk all!

[Pointing to her hair.

Those locks are well, and you are beauteous thus,
But with the dagger 't is, I have to do!

ANAEL
With mine!

DJABAL
Blood—Anael?

ANAEL
Djabal, 't is thy deed!
It must be! I had hoped to claim it mine—
Be worthy thee—but I must needs confess
'T was not I, but thyself ... not I have ... Djabal!
Speak to me!

DJABAL
Oh my punishment!

ANAEL
Speak to me
While I can speak! touch me, despite the blood!
When the command passed from thy soul to mine,
I went, fire leading me, muttering of thee,
And the approaching exaltation,—"make
One sacrifice!" I said,—and he sat there,
Bade me approach; and, as I did approach,
Thy fire with music burst into my brain.
'T was but a moment's work, thou saidst—perchance
It may have been so! Well, it is thy deed!

DJABAL
It is my deed!

ANAEL
His blood all this!—this! and ...
And more! Sustain me, Djabal! Wait not—now
Let flash thy glory! Change thyself and me!
It must be! Ere the Druses flock to us!
At least confirm me! Djabal, blood gushed forth—
He was our tyrant—but I looked he'd fall
Prone as asleep—why else is death called sleep?
Sleep? He bent o'er his breast! 'T is sin, I know,—
Punish me, Djabal, but wilt thou let him?
Be it thou that punishest, not he—who creeps
On his red breast—is here! 'T is the small groan
Of a child—no worse! Bestow the new life, then!
Too swift it cannot be, too strange, surpassing!

[Following him up as he retreats.

Now! Change us both! Change me and change thou!

DJABAL [Sinks on his knees]
Thus!
Behold my change! You have done nobly. I!—

ANAEL
Can Hakeem kneel?

DJABAL
No Hakeem, and scarce Djabal!
I have dealt falsely, and this woe is come.
No—hear me ere scorn blast me! Once and ever,
The deed is mine! Oh think upon the past!

ANAEL [To herself]
Did I strike once, or twice, or many times?

DJABAL
I came to lead my tribe where, bathed in glooms,
Doth Bahumid the Renovator sleep:
Anael, I saw my tribe: I said, "Without
A miracle this cannot be"—I said
"Be there a miracle!"—for I saw you!

ANAEL
His head lies south the portal!

DJABAL
—Weighed with this
The general good, how could I choose my own?
What matter was my purity of soul?
Little by little I engaged myself—
Heaven would accept me for its instrument,
I hoped: I said Heaven had accepted me!

ANAEL
Is it this blood breeds dreams in me?—Who said
You were not Hakeem? And your miracles—
The fire that plays innocuous round your form?

[Again changing her whole manner.

Ah, thou wouldst try me—thou art Hakeem still!

DJABAL
Woe—woe! As if the Druses of the Mount
(Scarce Arabs, even there, but here, in the Isle,
Beneath their former selves) should comprehend
The subtle lore of Europe! A few secrets
That would not easily affect the meanest
Of the crowd there, could wholly subjugate
The best of our poor tribe. Again that eye?

ANAEL [After a pause springs to his neck]
Djabal,
in this there can be no deceit!
Why, Djabal, were you human only,—think,
Maani is but human, Khalil human,
Loys is human even—did their words
Haunt me, their looks pursue me? Shame on you
So to have tried me! Rather, shame on me
So to need trying! Could I, with the Prefect
And the blood, there—could I see only you?
—Hang by your neck over this gulf of blood?
Speak, I am saved! Speak, Djabal! Am I saved?

[As **DJABAL** slowly unclasps her arms, and puts her silently from him.

Hakeem would save me! Thou art Djabal! Crouch!
Bow to the dust, thou basest of our kind!
The pile of thee, I reared up to the cloud—
Full, midway, of our fathers' trophied tombs,
Based on the living rock, devoured not by
The unstable desert's jaws of sand,—falls prone!
Fire, music, quenched: and now thou liest there
A ruin, obscene creatures will moan through!
—Let us come, Djabal!

DJABAL
Whither come?

ANAEL
At once—
Lest so it grow intolerable. Come!
Will I not share it with thee? Best at once!
So, feel less pain! Let them deride,—thy tribe
Now trusting in thee,—Loys shall deride!
Come to them, hand in hand, with me!

DJABAL
Where come?

ANAEL
Where?—to the Druses thou hast wronged! Confess,
Now that the end is gained—(I love thee now—)
That thou hast so deceived them—(perchance love thee
Better than ever!) Come, receive their doom
Of infamy! Oh, best of all I love thee!
Shame with the man, no triumph with the God,
Be mine! Come!

DJABAL
Never! More shame yet? and why?
Why? You have called this deed mine—it is mine!
And with it I accept its circumstance.
How can I longer strive with fate? The past
Is past: my false life shall henceforth show true.
Hear me! The argosies touch land by this;
They bear us to fresh scenes and happier skies:
What if we reign together?—if we keep
Our secret for the Druses' good?—by means
Of even their superstition, plant in them
New life? I learn from Europe: all who seek
Man's good must awe man, by such means as these.
We two will be divine to them—we are!
All great works in this world spring from the ruins
Of greater projects—ever, on our earth,
Babels men block out, Babylons they build.
I wrest the weapon from your hand! I claim
The deed! Retire! You have my ring—you bar
All access to the Nuncio till the forces
From Venice land!

ANAEL
Thou wilt feign Hakeem then?

DJABAL [Putting the Tiara of Hakeem, on his head]
And from this moment that I dare ope wide
Eyes that till now refused to see, begins
My true dominion: for I know myself,
And what am I to personate. No word?

[**ANAEL** goes.

'T is come on me at last! His blood on her—
What memories will follow that! Her eye,
Her fierce distorted lip and ploughed black brow!
Ah, fool! Has Europe then so poorly tamed
The Syrian blood from out thee? Thou, presume
To work in this foul earth by means not foul?
Scheme, as for heaven,—but, on the earth, be glad
If a least ray like heaven's be left thee!
Thus
I shall be calm—in readiness—no way
Surprised.

[A noise without.

This should be Khalil and my Druses.
Venice is come then! Thus I grasp thee, sword!
Druses, 't is Hakeem saves you! In! Behold
Your Prefect!

[Enter **LOYS**. **DJABAL** hides the khandjar in his robe.

LOYS
Oh, well found, Djabal!—but no time for words.
You know who waits there?

[Pointing to the alcove.

Well!—and that 't is there
He meets the Nuncio? Well? Now, a surprise—
He there—

DJABAL
I know—

LOYS
—is now no mortal's lord,
Is absolutely powerless—call him, dead—
He is no longer Prefect—you are Prefect!
Oh, shrink not! I do nothing in the dark,
Nothing unworthy Breton blood, believe!
I understood at once your urgency
That I should leave this isle for Rhodes; I felt
What you were loath to speak—your need of help.
I have fulfilled the task, that earnestness
Imposed on me: have, face to face, confronted
The Prefect in full Chapter, charged on him
The enormities of his long rule; he stood
Mute, offered no defence, no crime denied.
On which, I spoke of you, and of your tribe,
Your faith so like our own, and all you urged
Of old to me—I spoke, too, of your goodness,
Your patience—brief, I hold henceforth the Isle
In charge, am nominally lord,—but you,
You are associated in my rule—
Are the true Prefect! Ay, such faith had they
In my assurance of your loyalty
(For who insults an imbecile old man?)
That we assume the Prefecture this hour!
You gaze at me? Hear greater wonders yet—
I cast down all the fabric I have built!
These Knights, I was prepared to worship ... but
Of that another time; what's now to say,

Is—I shall never be a Knight! Oh, Djabal,
Here first I throw all prejudice aside,
And call you brother! I am Druse like you:
My wealth, my friends, my power, are wholly yours,
Your people's, which is now my people: for
There is a maiden of your tribe, I love—
She loves me—Khalil's sister—

DJABAL
Anael?

LOYS
Start you?
Seems what I say, unknightly? Thus it chanced:
When first I came, a novice, to the isle ...

[Enter one of the **NUNCIO'S GUARDS** from the alcove.

GUARD
Oh horrible! Sir Loys! Here is Loys!
And here—

[Others enter from the alcove.

[Pointing to **DJABAL**.

Secure him, bind him—this is he!

[They surround **DJABAL**.

LOYS
Madmen—what is 't you do? Stand from my friend,
And tell me!

GUARD
Thou canst have no part in this—
Surely no part! But slay him not! The Nuncio
Commanded, slay him not!

LOYS
Speak, or ...

GUARD
The Prefect
Lies murdered there by him thou dost embrace.

LOYS
By Djabal? Miserable fools! How Djabal?

[A **GUARD** lifts **DJABAL'S** robe; **DJABAL** flings down the khandjar.

LOYS [After a pause]
Thou hast received some insult worse than all,
Some outrage not to be endured—
[To the **GUARDS**]
Stand back!
He is my friend—more than my friend! Thou hast
Slain him upon that provocation!

GUARD
No!
No provocation! 'T is a long devised
Conspiracy: the whole tribe is involved.
He is their Khalif—'t is on that pretence—
Their mighty Khalif who died long ago,
And now comes back to life and light again!
All is just now revealed, I know not how,
By one of his confederates—who, struck
With horror at this murder, first apprised
The Nuncio. As 't was said, we find this Djabal
Here where we take him.

DJABAL [Aside]
Who broke faith with me?

LOYS [To **DJABAL**]
Hear'st thou? Speak! Till thou speak I
keep off these,
Or die with thee. Deny this story! Thou
A Khalif, an impostor? Thou, my friend,
Whose tale was of an inoffensive tribe,
With ... but thou know'st—on that tale's truth I pledged
My faith before the Chapter: what art thou?

DJABAL
Loys, I am as thou hast heard. All 's true!
No more concealment! As these tell thee, all
Was long since planned. Our Druses are enough
To crush this handful: the Venetians land
Even now in our behalf. Loys, we part!
Thou, serving much, wouldst fain have served me more;
It might not be. I thank thee. As thou hearest,
We are a separated tribe: farewell!

LOYS
Oh, where will truth be found now? Canst thou so

Belie the Druses? Do they share thy crime?
Those thou professest of our Breton stock,
Are partners with thee? Why, I saw but now
Khalil, my friend—he spoke with me—no word
Of this! and Anael—whom I love, and who
Loves me—she spoke no word of this!

DJABAL
Poor boy!
Anael, who loves thee? Khalil, fast thy friend?
We, offsets from a wandering Count of Dreux?
No: older than the oldest, princelier
Than Europe's princeliest race, our tribe: enough
For thine, that on our simple faith we found
A monarchy to shame your monarchies
At their own trick and secret of success.
The child of this our tribe shall laugh upon
The palace-step of him whose life ere night
Is forfeit, as that child shall know, and yet
Shall laugh there! What, we Druses wait forsooth
The kind interposition of a boy
—Can only save ourselves if thou concede?
—Khalil admire thee? He is my right hand,
My delegate!—Anael accept thy love?
She is my bride!

LOYS
Thy bride? She one of them?

DJABAL
My bride!

LOYS
And she retains her glorious eyes!
She, with those eyes, has shared this miscreant's guilt!
Ah—who but she directed me to find
Djabal within the Prefect's chamber? Khalil
Bade me seek Djabal there, too! All is truth!
What spoke the Prefect worse of them than this?
Did the Church ill to institute long since
Perpetual warfare with such serpentry?
And I—have I desired to shift my part,
Evade my share in her design? 'T is well!

DJABAL
Loys, I wronged thee—but unwittingly:
I never thought there was in thee a virtue
That could attach itself to what thou deemest

A race below thine own. I wronged thee, Loys,
But that is over: all is over now,
Save the protection I ensure against
My people's anger. By their Khalif's side,
Thou art secure and may'st depart: so, come!

LOYS
Thy side? I take protection at thy hand?

[Enter other **GUARDS**.

GUARDS
Fly with him! Fly, Sir Loys! 'T is too true!
And only by his side thou may'st escape!
The whole tribe is in full revolt: they flock
About the palace—will be here—on thee—
And there are twenty of us, we the Guards
O' the Nuncio, to withstand them! Even we
Had stayed to meet our death in ignorance,
But that one Druse, a single faithful Druse,
Made known the horror to the Nuncio. Fly!
The Nuncio stands aghast. At least let us
Escape thy wrath, O Hakeem! We are naught
In thy tribe's persecution!
[To **LOYS**]
Keep by him!
They hail him Hakeem, their dead Prince returned:
He is their God, they shout, and at his beck
Are life and death!

[**LOYS**, springing at the khandjar **DJABAL** had thrown down, seizes him by the throat.

LOYS
Thus by his side am I!
Thus I resume my knighthood and its warfare,
Thus end thee, miscreant, in thy pride of place!
Thus art thou caught. Without, thy dupes may cluster.
Friends aid thee, foes avoid thee,—thou art Hakeem,
How say they?—God art thou! but also here
Is the least, youngest, meanest the Church calls
Her servant, and his single arm avails
To aid her as she lists. I rise, and thou
Art crushed! Hordes of thy Druses flock without:
Here thou hast me, who represent the Cross,
Honor and Faith, 'gainst Hell, Mahound and thee.
Die!

[**DJABAL** remains calm.

Implore my mercy, Hakeem, that my scorn
May help me! Nay, I cannot ply thy trade;
I am no Druse, no stabber: and thine eye,
Thy form, are too much as they were—my friend
Had such! Speak! Beg for mercy at my foot!

[**DJABAL** still silent.

Heaven could not ask so much of me—not, sure,
So much! I cannot kill him so!

[After a pause.

Thou art
Strong in thy cause, then—dost outbrave us, then.
Heardst thou that one of thine accomplices,
Thy very people, has accused thee? Meet
His charge! Thou hast not even slain the Prefect
As thy own vile creed warrants. Meet that Druse!
Come with me and disprove him—be thou tried
By him, nor seek appeal! Promise me this,
Or I will do God's office! What, shalt thou
Boast of assassins at thy beck, yet truth
Want even an executioner? Consent,
Or I will strike—look in my face—I will!

DJABAL
Give me again my khandjar, if thou darest!

[**LOYS** gives it.

Let but one Druse accuse me, and I plunge
This home. A Druse betray me? Let us go!
[Aside] Who has betrayed me?

[Shouts without.

Hearest thou? I hear
No plainer than long years ago I heard
That shout—but in no dream now! They return!
Wilt thou be leader with me, Loys? Well!

ACT V

The uninitiated **DRUSES**, filling the hall tumultuously, and speaking together.

Here flock we, obeying the summons. Lo,
Hakeem hath appeared, and the Prefect is
dead, and we return to Lebanon! My manufacture
of goats' fleece must, I doubt, soon fall
away there. Come, old Nasif—link thine arm
in mine—we fight, if needs be. Come, what
is a great fight-word?—"Lebanon?" (My
daughter—my daughter!)—But is Khalil to
have the office of Hamza?—Nay, rather, if he
be wise, the monopoly of henna and cloves.
Where is Hakeem?—The only prophet I ever
saw, prophesied at Cairo once, in my youth: a
little black Copht, dressed all in black too,
with a great stripe of yellow cloth flapping
down behind him like the back-fin of a water-serpent.
Is this he? Biamrallah! Biamreh!
HAKEEM!

[Enter the **NUNCIO**, with **GUARDS**.

NUNCIO [To his **ATTENDANTS**]
Hold both, the sorcerer and
this accomplice
Ye talk of, that accuseth him! And tell
Sir Loys he is mine, the Church's hope:
Bid him approve himself our Knight indeed!
Lo, this black disemboguing of the Isle!
[To the **DRUSES**]
Ah, children, what a sight for these old eyes
That kept themselves alive this voyage through
To smile their very last on you! I came
To gather one and all you wandering sheep
Into my fold, as though a father came ...
As though, in coming, a father should ...
[To his **GUARDS**]
(Ten, twelve
—Twelve guards of you, and not an outlet? None?
The wizards stop each avenue? Keep close!)
[To the **DRUSES**]
As if one came to a son's house, I say,
So did I come—no guard with me—to find ...
Alas—alas!

A DRUSE
Who is the old man?

ANOTHER

Oh, ye are to shout!
Children, he styles you.

OTHER DRUSES
Ay, the Prefect's slain!
Glory to the Khalif, our Father!

NUNCIO
Even so!
I find (ye prompt aright) your father slain!
While most he plotted for your good, that father
(Alas, how kind, ye never knew)—lies slain!
[Aside.] (And hell's worm gnaw the glozing knave—with me,
For being duped by his cajoleries!
Are these the Christians? These the docile crew
My bezants went to make me Bishop o'er?)
[To his **ATTENDANTS**, who whisper]
What say ye does this wizard style himself?
Hakeem? Biamrallah? The third Fatemite?
What is this jargon? He—the insane Khalif,
Dead near three hundred years ago, come back
In flesh and blood again?

OTHER DRUSES
He mutters! Hear ye?
He is blaspheming Hakeem. The old man
Is our dead Prefect's friend. Tear him!

NUNCIO
Ye dare not!
I stand here with my five-and-seventy years,
The Patriarch's power behind me, God's above!
Those years have witnessed sin enough; ere now
Misguided men arose against their lords,
And found excuse; but ye, to be enslaved
By sorceries, cheats—alas! the same tricks, tried
On my poor children in this nook o' the earth,
Could triumph, that have been successively
Exploded, laughed to scorn, all nations through:
"Romaioi, Ioudaioite kai proselutoi,
Cretes and Arabians,"—you are duped the last.
Said I, refrain from tearing me? I pray ye
Tear me! Shall I return to tell the Patriarch
That so much love was wasted—every gift
Rejected, from his benison I brought,
Down to the galley-full of bezants, sunk
An hour since at the harbor's mouth, by that ...
That ... never will I speak his hated name!

[To his **SERVANTS**]
What was the name his fellow slip-fetter
Called their arch-wizard by?

[They whisper.

Oh, Djabal was't?

OTHER DRUSES
But how a sorcerer? false wherein?

NUNCIO
(Ay, Djabal!)
How false? Ye know not, Djabal has confessed ...
Nay, that by tokens found on him we learn ...
What I sailed hither solely to divulge—
How by his spells the demons were allured
To seize you: not that these be aught save lies
And mere illusions. Is this clear? I say,
By measures such as these, he would have led you
Into a monstrous ruin: follow ye?
Say, shall ye perish for his sake, my sons?

OTHER DRUSES
Hark ye!

NUNCIO
—Be of one privilege amerced?
No! Infinite the Patriarch's mercies are!
No! With the Patriarch's license, still I bid
Tear him to pieces who misled you! Haste!

OTHER DRUSES
The old man's beard shakes, and his eyes are white fire!
After all, I know nothing of Djabal beyond what Karshook says; he knows but what Khalil says, who
knows just what Djabal says himself. Now, the little Copht Prophet, I saw at Cairo in my youth, began by
promising each bystander three full measures of wheat ...

[Enter **KHALIL** and the initiated **DRUSES**.

KHALIL
Venice and her deliverance are at hand:
Their fleet stands through the harbor! Hath he slain
The Prefect yet? Is Djabal's change come yet?

NUNCIO [To **ATTENDANTS**]
What's this of Venice? Who's this boy?

[**ATTENDANTS** whisper.

One Khalil?
Djabal's accomplice, Loys called, but now,
The only Druse, save Djabal's self, to fear?
[To the **DRUSES**]
I cannot hear ye with these aged ears;
Is it so? Ye would have my troops assist?
Doth he abet him in his sorceries?
Down with the cheat, guards, as my children bid!

[They spring at **KHALIL**; as he beats them back.

Stay! No more bloodshed! Spare deluded youth!
Whom seek'st thou? (I will teach him)—whom, my child?
Thou know'st not what these know, what these declare.
I am an old man, as thou seest—have done
With life; and what should move me but the truth?
Art thou the only fond one of thy tribe?
'T is I interpret for thy tribe!

KHALIL
Oh, this
Is the expected Nuncio! Druses, hear—
Endure ye this? Unworthy to partake
The glory Hakeem gains you! While I speak,
The ships touch land: who makes for Lebanon?
They plant the wingèd lion in these halls!

NUNCIO [Aside]
If it be true! Venice? Oh, never true!
Yet Venice would so gladly thwart our Knights,
So fain get footing here, stand close by Rhodes!
Oh, to be duped this way!

KHALIL
Ere he appear
And lead you gloriously, repent, I say!

NUNCIO [Aside]
Nor any way to stretch the arch-wizard stark
Ere the Venetians come? Cut off the head,
The trunk were easily stilled.
[To the **DRUSES**]
He? Bring him forth!
Since so you needs will have it, I assent!
You 'd judge him, say you, on the spot?—confound
The sorcerer in his very circle? Where 's

Our short black-bearded sallow friend who swore
He 'd earn the Patriarch's guerdon by one stab?
Bring Djabal forth at once!

OTHER DRUSES
Ay, bring him forth!
The Patriarch drives a trade in oil and silk,
And we 're the Patriarch's children—true men, we!
Where is the glory? Show us all the glory!

KHALIL
You dare not so insult him! What, not see ...
(I tell thee, Nuncio, these are uninstructed,
Untrusted—they know nothing of our Khalif!)
—Not see that if he lets a doubt arise
'T is but to give yourselves the chance of seeming
To have some influence in your own return!
That all may say ye would have trusted him
Without the all-convincing glory—ay,
And did! Embrace the occasion, friends! For, think—
What wonder when his change takes place? But now
For your sakes, he should not reveal himself.
No—could I ask and have, I would not ask
The change yet!

[Enter **DJABAL** and **LOYS**.

Spite of all, reveal thyself!
I had said, pardon them for me—for Anael—
For our sakes pardon these besotted men—
Ay, for thine own—they hurt not thee! Yet now
One thought swells in me and keeps down all else.
This Nuncio couples shame with thee, has called
Imposture thy whole course, all bitter things
Has said: he is but an old fretful man!
Hakeem—nay, I must call thee Hakeem now—
Reveal thyself! See! Where is Anael? See!

LOYS [To **DJABAL**]
Here are thy people! Keep thy word to me!

DJABAL
Who of my people hath accused me?

NUNCIO
So!
So this is Djabal, Hakeem, and what not?
A fit deed, Loys, for thy first Knight's day!

May it be augury of thy after-life!
Ever prove truncheon of the Church as now
That, Nuncio of the Patriarch, having charge
Of the Isle here, I claim thee

[Turning to **DJABAL**]

—as these bid me,
Forfeit for murder done thy lawful prince,
Thou conjurer that peep'st and mutterest!
Why should I hold thee from their hands? (Spells, children?
But hear how I dispose of all his spells!)
Thou art a prophet?—wouldst entice thy tribe
From me?—thou workest miracles? (Attend!
Let him but move me with his spells!) I, Nuncio ...

DJABAL
... Which how thou camest to be, I say not now,
Though I have also been at Stamboul, Luke!
Ply thee with spells, forsooth! What need of spells?
If Venice, in her Admiral's person, stoop
To ratify thy compact with her foe,
The Hospitallers, for this Isle—withdraw
Her warrant of the deed which reinstates
My people in their freedom, tricked away
By him I slew,—refuse to convoy us
To Lebanon and keep the Isle we leave—
Then will be time to try what spells can do!
Dost thou dispute the Republic's power?

NUNCIO
Lo ye!
He tempts me too, the wily exorcist!
No! The renowned Republic was and is
The Patriarch's friend: 't is not for courting Venice
That I—that these implore thy blood of me!
Lo ye, the subtle miscreant! Ha, so subtle?
Ye Druses, hear him! Will ye be deceived?
How he evades me! Where 's the miracle
He works? I bid him to the proof—fish up
Your galley full of bezants that he sank!
That were a miracle! One miracle!
Enough of trifling, for it chafes my years.
I am the Nuncio, Druses! I stand forth
To save you from the good Republic's rage
When she shall find her fleet was summoned here
To aid the mummeries of a knave like this!

[As the **DRUSES** hesitate, his **ATTENDANTS** whisper.

Ah, well suggested! Why, we hold the while
One who, his close confederate till now,
Confesses Diabal at the last a cheat,
And every miracle a cheat! Who throws me
His head? I make three offers, once I offer,—
And twice ...

DJABAL
Let who moves perish at my foot!

KHALIL
Thanks, Hakeem, thanks! Oh, Anael, Maani,
Why tarry they?

OTHER DRUSES [To each other]
He can! He can! Live fire—
[To the **NUNCIO**]
I say he can, old man! Thou know'st him not.
Live fire like that thou seest now in his eyes,
Plays fawning round him. See! The change begins!
All the brow lightens as he lifts his arm!
Look not at me! It was not I!

DJABAL
What Druse
Accused me, as he saith? I bid each bone
Crumble within that Druse! None, Loys, none
Of my own people, as thou said'st, have raised
A voice against me.

NUNCIO [Aside]
Venice to come! Death!

DJABAL [Continuing]
Confess and go unscathed, however false!
Seest thou my Druses, Luke? I would submit
To thy pure malice did one Druse confess!
How said I, Loys?

NUNCIO [To his **ATTENDANTS** who whisper]
Ah, ye counsel so?
[Aloud] Bring in the witness, then, who, first of all,
Disclosed the treason! Now I have thee, wizard!
Ye hear that? If one speaks, he bids you tear him
Joint after joint: well then, one does speak! One,
Befooled by Djabal, even as yourselves,

But who hath voluntarily proposed
To expiate, by confessing thus, the fault
Of having trusted him.

[They bring in a veiled **DRUSE**.

LOYS
Now, Djabal, now!

NUNCIO
Friend, Djabal fronts thee! Make a ring, sons. Speak!
Expose this Djabal—what he was, and how;
The wiles he used, the aims he cherished; all,
Explicitly as late 't was spoken to these
My servants: I absolve and pardon thee.

LOYS
Thou hast the dagger ready, Djabal?

DJABAL
Speak, Recreant!

OTHER DRUSES
Stand back, fool! farther! Suddenly
You shall see some huge serpent glide from under
The empty vest, or down will thunder crash!
Back, Khalil!

KHALIL
I go back? Thus go I back!
[To **ANAEL**]
Unveil! Nay, thou shalt face the Khalif! Thus!

[He tears away **ANAEL'S** veil; **DJABAL** folds his arms and bows his head; the **DRUSES** fall back; LOYS
springs from the side of **DJABAL** and the **NUNCIO**.

LOYS
Then she was true—she only of them all!
True to her eyes—may keep those glorious eyes,
And now be mine, once again mine! Oh, Anael!
Dared I think thee a partner in his crime—
That blood could soil that hand? nay, 't is mine—Anael,
—Not mine?—Who offer thee before all these
My heart, my sword, my name—so thou wilt say
That Djabal, who affirms thou art his bride,
Lies—say but that he lies!

DJABAL

Thou, Anael?

LOYS
Nay, Djabal, nay, one chance for me—the last!
Thou hast had every other; thou hast spoken
Days, nights, what falsehood listed thee—let me
Speak first now; I will speak now!

NUNCIO
Loys, pause!
Thou art the Duke's son, Bretagne's choicest stock,
Loys of Dreux, God's sepulchre's first sword:
This wilt thou spit on, this degrade, this trample
To earth?

LOYS [To **ANAEL**]
Who had foreseen that one day, Loys
Would stake these gifts against some other good
In the whole world? I give them thee! I would
My strong will might bestow real shape on them,
That I might see, with my own eyes, thy foot
Tread on their very neck! 'T is not by gifts
I put aside this Djabal: we will stand—
We do stand, see, two men! Djabal, stand forth!
Who's worth her, I or thou? I—who for Anael
Uprightly, purely kept my way, the long
True way—left thee each by-path, boldly lived
Without the lies and blood,—or thou, or thou?
Me! love me, Anael! Leave the blood and him!
[To **DJABAL**]
Now speak—now, quick on this that I have said,—
Thou with the blood, speak if thou art a man!

DJABAL [To **ANAEL**]
And was it thou betrayedst me? 'T is well!
I have deserved this of thee, and submit.
Nor 't is much evil thou inflictest: life
Ends here. The cedars shall not wave for us:
For there was crime, and must be punishment.
See fate! By thee I was seduced, by thee
I perish: yet do I—can I repent?
I with my Arab instinct, thwarted ever
By my Frank policy,—and with, in turn,
My Frank brain, thwarted by my Arab heart—
While these remained in equipoise, I lived
—Nothing; had either been predominant,
As a Frank schemer or an Arab mystic,
I had been something;—now, each has destroyed

The other—and behold, from out their crash,
A third and better nature rises up—
My mere man's-nature! And I yield to it:
I love thee, I who did not love before!

ANAEL
Djabal!

DJABAL
It seemed love, but it was not love:
How could I love while thou adoredst me?
Now thou despisest, art above me so
Immeasurably! Thou, no other, doomest
My death now; this my steel shall execute
Thy judgment; I shall feel thy hand in it!
Oh, luxury to worship, to submit,
Transcended, doomed to death by thee!

ANAEL
My Djabal!

DJABAL
Dost hesitate? I force thee then! Approach,
Druses! for I am out of reach of fate;
No further evil waits me. Speak the doom!
Hear, Druses, and hear, Nuncio, and hear, Loys!

ANAEL
HAKEEM!

[She falls dead.

[The **DRUSES** scream, grovelling before him.

OTHER DRUSES
Ah, Hakeem!—not on me thy wrath!
Biamrallah, pardon! never doubted I!
Ha, dog, how sayest thou?

[They surround and seize the **NUNCIO** and his **GUARDS**. **LOYS** flings himself upon the body of **ANAEL**, on which **DJABAL** continues to gaze as stupefied.

NUNCIO
Caitiffs! Have ye eyes?
Whips, racks should teach you! What, his fools? his dupes?
Leave me! unhand me!

KHALIL [Approaching **DJABAL** timidly]

Save her for my sake!
She was already thine; she would have shared
To-day thine exaltation: think, this day
Her hair was plaited thus because of thee!
Yes, feel the soft bright hair—feel!

NUNCIO [Struggling with those who have seized him]
What, because
His leman dies for him? You think it hard
To die? Oh, would you were at Rhodes, and choice
Of deaths should suit you!

KHALIL [Bending over **ANAEL'S** body]
Just restore her life!
So little does it! there—the eyelids tremble!
'T was not my breath that made them: and the lips
Move of themselves. I could restore her life!
Hakeem, we have forgotten—have presumed
On our free converse: we are better taught.
See, I kiss—how I kiss thy garment's hem
For her! She kisses it—Oh, take her deed
In mine! Thou dost believe now, Anael?—See,
She smiles! Were her lips open o'er the teeth
Thus, when I spoke first? She believes in thee!
Go not without her to the cedars, lord!
Or leave us both—I cannot go alone!
I have obeyed thee, if I dare so speak:
Hath Hakeem thus forgot all Djabal knew?
Thou feelest then my tears fall hot and fast
Upon thy hand, and yet thou speakest not?
Ere the Venetian trumpet sound—ere thou
Exalt thyself, O Hakeem! save thou her!

NUNCIO
And the accursed Republic will arrive
And find me in their toils—dead, very like,
Under their feet!
What way—not one way yet
To foil them? None?

[Observing **DJABAL'S** face.

What ails the Khalif? Ah,
That ghastly face! A way to foil them yet!
[To the **DRUSES**] Look to your Khalif, Druses! Is that face
God Hakeem's? Where is triumph,—where is ... what
Said he of exaltation—hath he promised
So much to-day? Why then, exalt thyself!

Cast off that husk, thy form, set free thy soul
In splendor! Now, bear witness! here I stand—
I challenge him exalt himself, and I
Become, for that, a Druse like all of you!

THE DRUSES
Exalt thyself! Exalt thyself, O Hakeem!

DJABAL [Advances]
I can confess now all from first to last.
There is no longer shame for me. I am ...

[Here the Venetian trumpet sounds: the **DRUSES** shout, **DJABAL'S** eye catches the expression of those about him, and, as the old dream comes back, he is again confident and inspired.

—Am I not Hakeem? And ye would have crawled
But yesterday within these impure courts
Where now ye stand erect! Not grand enough?
—What more could be conceded to such beasts
As all of you, so sunk and base as you,
Than a mere man? A man among such beasts
Was miracle enough: yet him you doubt,
Him you forsake, him fain would you destroy—
With the Venetians at your gate, the Nuncio
Thus—(see the baffled hypocrite!) and, best,
The Prefect there!

OTHER DRUSES
No, Hakeem, ever thine!

NUNCIO
He lies—and twice he lies—and thrice he lies!
Exalt thyself, Mahound! Exalt thyself!

DJABAL
Druses! we shall henceforth be far away—
Out of mere mortal ken—above the cedars—
But we shall see ye go, hear ye return,
Repeopling the old solitudes,—through thee,
My Khalil! Thou art full of me: I fill
Thee full—my hands thus fill thee! Yester-eve,
—Nay, but this morn, I deemed thee ignorant
Of all to do, requiring word of mine
To teach it: now, thou hast all gifts in one,
With truth and purity go other gifts,
All gifts come clustering to that. Go, lead
My people home whate'er betide!

[Turning to the **DRUSES**]

Ye take
This Khalil for my delegate? To him
Bow as to me? He leads to Lebanon—
Ye follow?

OTHER DRUSES
We follow! Now exalt thyself!

DJABAL [Raises **LOYS**]
Then to thee, Loys! How I wronged thee, Loys!
Yet, wronged, no less thou shalt have full revenge,
Fit for thy noble self, revenge—and thus.
Thou, loaded with such wrongs, the princely soul,
The first sword of Christ's sepulchre—thou shalt
Guard Khalil and my Druses home again!
Justice, no less, God's justice and no more,
For those I leave!—to seeking this, devote
Some few days out of thy Knight's brilliant life:
And, this obtained them, leave their Lebanon,
My Druses' blessing in thine ears—(they shall
Bless thee with blessing sure to have its way)
—One cedar-blossom in thy ducal cap,
One thought of Anael in thy heart,—perchance,
One thought of him who thus, to bid thee speed,
His last word to the living speaks! This done,
Resume thy course, and, first amidst the first
In Europe, take my heart along with thee!
Go boldly, go serenely, go augustly—
What shall withstand thee then?

[He bends over **ANAEL**.

And last to thee!
Ah, did I dream I was to have, this day,
Exalted thee? A vain dream: hast thou not
Won greater exaltation? What remains
But press to thee, exalt myself to thee?
Thus I exalt myself, set free my soul!

[He stabs himself. As he falls, supported by **KHALIL** and **LOYS**, the **VENETIANS** enter; the **ADMIRAL** advances.

ADMIRAL
God and St. Mark for Venice! Plant the Lion!

[At the clash of the planted standard, the **DRUSES** shout, and move tumultuously forward, **LOYS** drawing his sword.

DJABAL [Leading them a few steps between **KHALIL** and **LOYS**]
On to the Mountain!
At the Mountain, Druses!

[Dies.

Robert Browning – A Short Biography

He is the equal of any Victorian Poet that could be mentioned. However, Browning continues to be in the shadow of Tennyson, Arnold, Hopkins, Morris and many others.

Robert Browning was born on May 7th, 1812 in Walworth in the parish of Camberwell, London. He was baptized on June 14th, 1812, at Lock's Fields Independent Chapel, York Street, Walworth.

Browning's early years were certainly very interesting. His mother was an excellent pianist and a very devout evangelical Christian. His father, who worked as a clerk at the Bank of England, was also an artist, scholar, antiquarian, and collector of books and pictures. Indeed, he amassed more than 6,000 volumes of rare books including works in Greek, Hebrew, Latin, French, Italian, and Spanish. For the young and curious Browning, it was a wonderful resource, added to which his father was a guiding force in his education.

Many accounts attest that Browning was already proficient at reading and writing by the age of five. He is said to have been a bright but anxious student and to have studied and learnt Latin, Greek, and French by the time he was fourteen. From fourteen to sixteen he was educated at home, tutored in music, drawing, dancing, and horsemanship. Certainly, language and the arts were two areas the young Browning both absorbed and pushed himself towards.

At the age of twelve he wrote a volume of Byronic verse he called Incondita, which his parents attempted to have published. The attempts were unsuccessful and, disappointed, Browning destroyed the work.

In 1825, a cousin gave Browning a collection of Percy Bysshe Shelley's poetry; Browning was so enamored with the poems that he asked for the rest of Shelley's works for his thirteenth birthday. In fact, Browning then went the extra mile, declaring himself to be both a vegetarian and an atheist in honour of his hero.

Intriguingly it seems that the rejection of his first volume didn't dim his appreciation of other poets, but it appears to have stopped him writing any poems between the ages of thirteen and twenty.

In 1828, Browning enrolled at the newly-opened University of London. He was uncomfortable with the experience and he soon left, anxious to read and absorb at his own pace.

His education which, overall is notably rambling and lacks a structure that many of his artistic contemporaries enjoyed, i.e. excellent public schooling and then a degree at Oxford or Cambridge, may present many of his critics with ammunition to criticize, but alternatively his hap-hazard education certainly contributed to many of the references that baffled both critics and his audience, but they tellingly show the breath and scale of what he could turn words too. What others would call obscure references were, to Browning, remarkably obvious.

Browning's early career was very promising. His long poem Pauline (of which only a fragment was ever finished and published) brought him to the attention of the Pre-Raphaelite master Dante Gabriel Rossetti and his difficult Paracelsus (published in 1835) was warmly admired by both Dickens and Wordsworth.

In the 1830s he met the actor William Macready and was encouraged to develop and turn his talents to the stage by writing verse drama. But these plays, including Strafford, which ran for five nights in 1837, and those contained within the Bells and Pomegranates series, were, for the most part, unsuccessful.

During this period Browning began to discover that his real talents lay in taking a single character and allowing that character to discover more about himself by revealing further personal aspects of himself in his speeches; the dramatic monologue. The techniques he developed through this—especially the use of diction, rhythm, and symbol—are regarded as his most important contribution to poetry. They would later influence such major poets of the 20th Century as Ezra Pound, T. S. Eliot, and Robert Frost.

By 1840, with the publication of Sordello, the tide turned somewhat. Many thought he was being deliberately obscure, opaque beyond measure and his poetry for the next decade or so was not eagerly acquired or talked about.

As Browning attempted to rehabilitate his career he began a relationship with Elizabeth Barrett in 1845. He had read her poems and, being totally charmed by their quality, was determined to meet her. The poetess was better known than the younger Browning but suffered from a debilitating illness and was also subject to the harsh behaviour of her over-bearing father. Nevertheless, the new couple were soon inseparable.

Her father, as he did with any of his children that married, disinherited her. Despite this she had some money from her own resources and sensing that the best outcome for both the relationship and her own health was to move abroad the couple did just that. After a private marriage at St Marylebone Parish Church, in September 1846, they journeyed to Europe to honeymoon in Paris.

Their new life now took them to Italy, first to Pisa and a little later to Florence. There they absorbed life and one another.

But in the short term the literary assault on Browning's work did not let up. He was now criticized by such patrician writers as Charles Kingsley for his abandonment of England for foreign lands. Browning could do little to answer these attacks except to compose with his pen and continue with his poetical journey.

The Browning's were well respected, and even famous. Elizabeth health began to improve, she grew stronger and in 1849, at the age of 43, between four miscarriages, she gave birth to a son, Robert Wiedeman Barrett Browning, whom they nicknamed "Penini" or "Pen",

Intriguingly despite his growing reputation and return to form as a poet he was more often than not known as 'Elizabeth Barrett's husband'.

Work flowed from his pen that was to ensure his reputation as one of England's leading poets. When his collection Men and Women was published in 1855 it contained some of his finest lines. It was dedicated to Elizabeth. Life had begun to smile handsome rewards upon the Brownings.

Victorian society was very much taken with all things spiritualist. It was not enough to have command of much of the globe through Empire, they wished to know and explore wherever they could. The spirit world beckoned their interest. Browning dissented from this view believing it was all a hoax and a fraud. Elizabeth, however, was inclined to believe and this caused several disagreements between the couple.

They attended a séance by Daniel Dunglas Home, in July 1855. (Home was a famous and clamored after Scottish physical medium with the reported ability to levitate and speak with the dead). It is said that during this séance a spirit face materialised. Home then claimed it was the face of Browning's son who had died in infancy. Browning seized the 'materialisation' which turned out to be Home's bare foot. Browning had never lost a son in infancy.

After the séance, Browning wrote an angry letter to The Times, in which he said: "the whole display of hands, spirit utterances etc., was a cheat and imposture."

The Browning's time in Italy were immensely rewarding years for both their personal and professional lives. Browning encouraged her to include Sonnets from the Portuguese in her published works, these beautiful poems are undoubtedly one of the highlights of English love poetry.

Elizabeth had become quite politicised during these years. Engrossed in Italian politics (which was continuing to slowly re-unify the country), she issued a small volume of political poems entitled Poems before Congress (1860) most of which were written to express her sympathy with the Italian cause after the earlier outbreak of The Second Italian Independence War in 1859. In England they caused uproar. Conservative magazines such as Blackwood's and the Saturday Review labelled her a fanatic. She dedicated the book to her husband.

But in 1861 tragedy struck.

The couple had spent the winter of 1860–61 in Rome when Elizabeth's health deteriorated again and they returned to Florence in early June. However, these turned out to be her final weeks. Only morphine would now still the pain. She died in Browning's arms on June 29th, 1861. Browning said that she died "smilingly, happily, and with a face like a girl's .... Her last word was .... "Beautiful".

Her burial took place in the nearby Protestant English Cemetery of Florence. The local people were deeply saddened, and shops closed their doors in grief and respect.

Browning and their son were obviously devastated. Unable to bear being in Florence without Elizabeth they soon returned to London to live at 19 Warwick Crescent, Maida Vale.

As he re-integrated himself back into the London literary scene he began to finally receive the proper praise, respect and reputation that his works deserved.

Browning went on to publish Dramatis Personæ (1864), and The Ring and the Book (1868–1869). The latter, based on an "old yellow book" which told of a seventeenth-century Italian murder trial, received wide and generous critical acclaim. Although by now he was in the twilight of a long and prolific career, that had achieved some notable ups and downs, he was respected and indeed renowned for his talents and works.

In 1878, he revisited Italy for the first time since Elizabeth's death. He would return there on several further occasions but never to Florence.

Such was the esteem he was held in that The Browning Society was founded in 1881. Although he had never obtained a degree (something that set him apart from many other Victorian poets) he was now awarded honorary degrees from Oxford University in 1882 and then the University of Edinburgh in 1884.

In 1887, Browning produced the major work of his later years, Parleyings with Certain People of Importance in Their Day. Browning now spoke with his own voice as he engaged in a series of dialogues with long-forgotten figures of literary, artistic, and philosophic history. Unfortunately, both the critics and public were completely baffled by this.

On April 7th, 1889 Browning attended a dinner party at the home of his friend, the artist Rudolf Lehmann. The highlight of which was a recording made on a wax cylinder on an Edison cylinder phonograph. On the recording, which still exists, Browning recites part of How They Brought the Good News from Ghent to Aix, and can even be heard apologising when he forgets the words.

The recording was first played in 1890 on the anniversary of his death, at a gathering of his admirers, it was said to be the first time anyone's voice 'had been heard from beyond the grave'.

His last work Asolando: Fancies and Facts (1889), returned to his brief and concise lyric verse that was so popular. It was published on the day of his death on December 12th, 1889, Robert Browning was at his son's home Ca' Rezzonico in Venice.

He was buried in Poets' Corner in Westminster Abbey; his grave lies immediately adjacent to that of Alfred Tennyson.

Among the many who have publicly acknowledged their literary debt to him are Henry James, Oscar Wilde, George Bernard Shaw, G. K. Chesterton, Ezra Pound, Jorge Luis Borges, and Vladimir Nabokov.

Robert Browning - A Concise Bibliography

Here follows a list of the plays and poetry volumes published during his lifetime. Poems of particular worth are noted from within those volumes.

Pauline: A Fragment of a Confession (1833)
Paracelsus (1835)
Strafford (play) (1837)
Sordello (1840)

Bells and Pomegranates No. I: Pippa Passes (play) (1841)
      The Year's at the Spring
Bells and Pomegranates No. II: King Victor and King Charles (play) (1842)
Bells and Pomegranates No. III: Dramatic Lyrics (1842)
      Porphyria's Lover
      Soliloquy of the Spanish Cloister
      My Last Duchess
      The Pied Piper of Hamelin
      Count Gismond
      Johannes Agricola in Meditation
Bells and Pomegranates No. IV: The Return of the Druses (play) (1843)
Bells and Pomegranates No. V: A Blot in the 'Scutcheon (play) (1843)
Bells and Pomegranates No. VI: Colombe's Birthday (play) (1844)
Bells and Pomegranates No. VII: Dramatic Romances and Lyrics (1845)
      The Laboratory
      How They Brought the Good News from Ghent to Aix
      The Bishop Orders His Tomb at Saint Praxed's Church
      The Lost Leader
      Home Thoughts from Abroad
      Meeting at Night
Bells and Pomegranates No. VIII: Luria and A Soul's Tragedy (plays) (1846)
Christmas-Eve and Easter-Day (1850)
An Essay on Percy Bysshe Shelley (essay) (1852)
Two Poems (1854)
Men and Women (1855)
      Love Among the Ruins
      A Toccata of Galuppi's
      Childe Roland to the Dark Tower Came
      Fra Lippo Lippi
      Andrea Del Sarto
      The Patriot
      The Last Ride Together
      Memorabilia
      Cleon
      How It Strikes a Contemporary
      The Statue and the Bust
      A Grammarian's Funeral
      An Epistle Containing the Strange Medical Experience of Karshish, the Arab Physician
      Bishop Blougram's Apology
      Master Hugues of Saxe-Gotha
      By the Fire-side
Dramatis Personae (1864)
      Caliban upon Setebos
      Rabbi Ben Ezra
      Abt Vogler
      Mr. Sludge, "The Medium"
      Prospice
      A Death in the Desert

The Ring and the Book (1868–69)
Balaustion's Adventure (1871)
Prince Hohenstiel-Schwangau, Saviour of Society (1871)
Fifine at the Fair (1872)
Red Cotton Night-Cap Country, or, Turf and Towers (1873)
Aristophanes' Apology (1875)
    Thamuris Marching
The Inn Album (1875)
Pacchiarotto, and How He Worked in Distemper (1876)
    Numpholeptos
The Agamemnon of Aeschylus (1877)
La Saisiaz and The Two Poets of Croisic (1878)
Dramatic Idylls (1879)
Dramatic Idylls: Second Series (1880)
    Pan and Luna
Jocoseria (1883)
Ferishtah's Fancies (1884)
Parleyings with Certain People of Importance in Their Day (1887)
Asolando (1889)
    Prologue
    Summum Bonum
    Bad Dreams III
    Flute-Music, with an Accompaniment
    Epilogue

www.ingramcontent.com/pod-product-compliance
Lightning Source LLC
Chambersburg PA
CBHW060050050426
42448CB00011B/2381